POOR RICHARD

AN ALMANACK

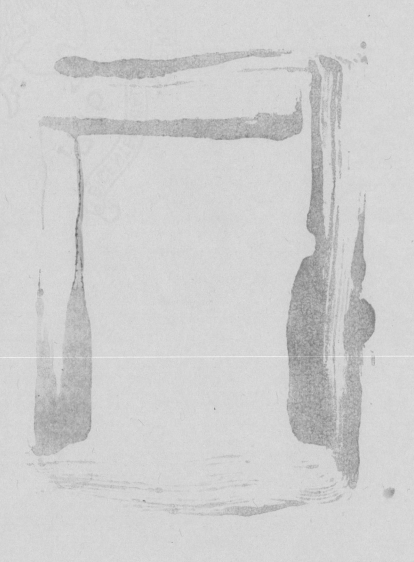

Benj. Franklin

POOR RICHARD

AN ALMANACK

BENJAMIN FRANKLIN

David McKay Company, Inc.

NEW YORK

Library of Congress Cataloging in Publication Data

Franklin, Benjamin, 1706-1790.
  Poor Richard.

  I. Title.
PS749.A6M3   818'.1'07   76-41594
ISBN 0-679-50655-1

INTRODUCTION

To begin with, Benjamin Franklin, Poor Richard, and Richard Saunders are all one and the same person. Or, to put it another way, Poor Richard and Richard Saunders are pseudonyms Ben Franklin used to add spice, life, and a comic touch to the annual almanacs he printed and published in Philadelphia from 1733 to 1758.

Who was the man who created the famous Poor Richard Saunders? Benjamin Franklin was as well known in his own day as he is today. His most famous achievement was, of course, the invention of the lightning rod, and proving that lightning was electricity. In fact, Franklin was the *only* American scientist of his day, and probably the world's first electrician. In addition to his scientific discoveries, Franklin was involved in many civic activities in the American colonies. He organized our first police force, and took the lead in street-lighting and the paving of city streets. He was president of our first Abolition Society, and was mainly responsible for the academy that was to become the University of Pennsylvania.

But while many Americans are aware of Benjamin Franklin's accomplishments, few people realize that they occurred in the later part of Franklin's career, when he was living on a three-hundred-acre farm he had retired to for a life of "leisure" in New Jersey. From the age of twenty-six to fifty-one, Franklin worked long, hard hours in his shop near the Philadelphia marketplace selling books, paper and parchment, perfumed soap, cheese, tea and coffee. And printing and selling a 24- to 36-page almanac, that, at its peak, reached best-seller sales of up to 10,000 copies a year, or one copy sold to one in every hundred people.

Franklin was not the only publisher of almanacs in his own day. In the early part of the eighteenth century, almanacs were known as "the one universal book of modern literature," the most popular of all publications in the American colonies. At that time the average almanac had a calendar, lists of places where a traveler could stay, descriptions of the highways, names of British kings and rulers of Europe, days for courts and fairs, dates of eclipses, prognostications about the weather, jokes, maxims, and aphorisms.

It was the quality of the aphorisms and general sayings in the Franklin-Saunders almanacs that distinguished them in their own day, causing them to become so popular and so widely quoted down to our own day. Poor Richard's thoughts on life and death, lawyers and doctors, pride and humility, drinking and eating, are as popular today as they were with this country's earliest settlers.

This book is a careful selection of the best sayings Benjamin Franklin printed in his almanacs over two hundred years ago. For the general reader's pleasure and edification, these famous sayings are presented here under the various subjects that Franklin wrote about. Ranging in tone from serious to silly, they are a perfect reflection of the rich and varied personality of their creator.

Any selection of Poor Richard's sayings would be incomplete without the hilarious prefaces he usually wrote to each almanac and addressed to his "most kind reader." The charm, humor, wit, and relevancy of Franklin's thoughts, written by the fictitious Richard Saunders, have not diminished over the two hundred years that separate Franklin's Colonial times from our own.

Contents

1 7 3 3

Courteous Reader,

I might in this place attempt to gain thy Favour, by declaring that I write Almanacks with no other View than that of the publick Good; but in this I should not be sincere; and Men are nowadays too wise to be deceived by Pretences how specious soever. The plain Truth of the Matter is, I am excessive poor, and my Wife, good Woman, is, I tell her, excessive proud; she cannot bear, she says, to sit spinning in her Shift of Tow, while I do nothing but gaze at the Stars; and has threatened more than once to burn all my Books and Rattling Traps (as she calls my Instruments) if I do not make some profitable Use of them for the good of the Family. The Printer has offer'd me some considerable share of the Profits, and I have thus begun to comply with my Dame's desire.

Indeed this Motive would have had Force enough to have made me publish my Almanack many Years since, had it not been overpower'd by my Regard for my good Friend and Fellow-Student, Mr. Titan Leeds, whose Interest I was extreamly unwilling to hurt: But this Obstacle (I am far from speaking it with Pleasure) is soon to be removed, since inexorable Death, who has never known to respect Merit, has already prepared the mortal Dart, the fatal Sister has already extended her destroying Shears, and that ingenious Man must soon be taken from us. He dies, by my Calculation made at his Request,

[1]

on Oct. 17. 1733 3ho. 29m. P.M. at the very instant of the ☌ of ☉ and ☿ : By his own Calculation he will survive till the 26th of the same Month. This small difference between us we have disputed whenever we have met these 9 years past; but at length he is inclined to agree with my Judgment; Which of us is most exact, a little Time will now determine. As therefore these Provinces may not longer expect to see any of his Performances after this Year, I think myself free to take up the Task, and request a share of the publick Encouragement; which I am more apt to hope for on this Account, that the Buyer of my Almanack may consider himself, not only as purchasing an useful Utensil, but as performing an Act of Charity, to his poor

Friend and Servant

R Saunders

DOCTORS & LAWYERS

He's a Fool that makes
his Doctor his Heir.

He's the best physician that knows the worthlessness
of the most medicines.

God heals
and the Doctor takes the Fee.

The Benifit of going to Law

Two Beggars travelling along,
One blind, the other lame,
Pick'd up an Oyster on the Way
To which they both laid claim:
The matter rose so high, that they
Resolv'd to go to Law,
as other richer Fools have done,
Who quarrel for a Straw.
A Lawyer took it strait in hand,
Who knew his business was,

[4]

To mind nor one not t'other side,
But make the best o'the Cause;
As always in the Law's the Case:
So he his Judgement gave,
and Lawyer-like he thus resolved
What each of them should have;
Blind Plantif, lame defendent, share
The Friendly Laws impartial care,
A Shell for him, a Shell for thee,
The Middle is the Lawyer's Fee.

God works wonders now & then:
Behold! a Lawyer, an honest man!

A Lawyer being sick and extream ill
Was moved by his friends to make his Will,
Which soon he did, gave all the Wealth he had
To frantic persons, lunatick and mad;
And to his friends this Reason did reveal
(That they might see with Equity he'd deal);
From Madmen's Hands I did my wealth receive,
Therefore that Wealth to Madmen's Hands I leave.

A countryman between two Lawyers,
is like a fish between two cats.

A good Lawyer, a bad Neighbour.

I know you Lawyers can, with Ease,
Twist words and Meanings as you please;
That language, by your Skill made pliant,
Will bend to favour ev'ry Client;

That 'tis the Fee directs the Sense
To make out either Side's Pretence:
When you persue the clearest Case,
You see it with a double Face.

A Farmer once made a Complaint to a Judge,
My Bull, if it please you, Sir, owing a Grudge,
Belike to one of your good Worship's Cattle,
Has slain him out-right in a mortal Battle:
I'm sorry at heart because of the Action,
And want to know how must be made Satisfaction.
Why, you must give me your Bull, that's plain,
Says the Judge, or pay me the Price of the Slain.
But I have mistaken the Case, Sir, says John,
The dead Bull I talk of, please you, 's my own:
And yours is the Beast that the Mischief has done.
The Judge soon replies with a serious Face:
Say you so; then this Accident alters the case.

On the Law

Nigh Neighbour to the Squire, poor Sam complain'd
of frequent Wrongs, but no Amends he gain'd.

Each Day his Gates thrown down, his Fence broke,
And injur'd still the more, the more he spoke.
At last, resolv'd his potent Foe to awe,
A Suit against him he began in Law;
Nine happy Terms thro' all the Forms he run,
Obtain'd his Cause—had Costs—and was undone.

1734

Courteous Readers,

Your kind and charitable Assistance last year, in purchasing so large an Impression of my Almanacks, has made my Circumstances much more easy in the World, and requires my grateful Acknowledgment. My wife has been Enabled to get a Pot of her own, and is no longer oblig'd to borrow one from a Neighbour; nor have we ever since been without something of our own to put in it. She has also got a pair of Shoes, two new Shifts, and a new warm Petticoat: and for my part, I have bought a second-hand coat, so good, that I am now not asham'd to go to Town to be seen there. These Things have render'd her Temper so much more pacifick than it us'd to be, that I may say, I have slept more, and more quietly within this past Year, than in the three foregoing Years put Together. Accept my Hearty Thanks therefore, and my sincere Wishes for your Health and Prosperity.

In the Preface to my last Almanack, I foretold the Death of my dear old Friend and Fellow-Student, the learned and ingenious *Mr. Titan Leeds,* which was to be on the 17th of *October,* 1733, 3h. 29m. *P.M.* at the very Instant of the ♂ of ☉ and ☿ . By his own Calculation he was to survive till the 26th of the same month, and expire in the Time of the Eclipse, near 11 a clock A.M. At which of these times he died, or whether he be really yet dead, I cannot at this Present writing positively assure my Readers; forasmuch as a Disorder in my own Family demanded

[8]

my Presence, and would not permit me, as I had intended, to be with him in his last Moments, to receive his last Embrace, to close his eyes, and do the duty of a friend in performing the last offices of the departed. Therefore it is that I cannot positively affirm whether he be dead or not; for the stars only show to the skillful what will happen in the natural and universal chain of causes and effects, but 'tis well known, that the events which would otherwise certainly happen at certain times in the course of nature, are sometimes set aside or postponed for wife and good reasons, by the immediate particular dispositions of Providence; which particular dispositions the stars can by no means discover or foreshow. There is however (and I cannot speak it without sorrow) there is the strongest *probability* that my dear friend is no more; for there appears in his name, as I am assured, an Almanack for the Year 1734, in which I am treated in a very gross and unhandsome manner; in which I am called "a false predicter, an Ignorant, a conceited scribbler, a fool, and a liar." Mr. Leeds was too well bred to use any man so indecently and so scurrilously, and moreover his esteem and affection for me was extraordinary, so that it is to be feared that pamflet may be only a contrivance of somebody or other who hopes perhaps to sell two or three years' Almanacks still, by the sole force and virtue of Mr. Leeds's name, but certainly, to put words into the mouth of a gentleman and a man of letters, against his friend, which the meanest and most scandalous of the people might be ashamed to utter even in a drunken quarrel, is an unpardonable injury to his memory, and an imposition upon the publick.

Mr. Leeds was not only profoundly skillful in the useful science he professed, but he was a man of exemplary sobriety, a most sincere friend, and an exact performer of his word. These valuable qualifications, with many others, so much endeared him to me, that although it should be so, that, contrary, to all probability, contrary to my prediction and his own, he might possibly be yet alive, yet my loss of honor as a prognosticator,

[9]

cannot afford me so much mortification, as his life, health and safety would give me joy and satisfaction. I am,

Courteous and kind Reader,

Your Poor Friend and Servant,

October 30, 1733.   R. SAUNDERS

LOVE

My neighbour H——y by his pleasing tongue,
Hath won a girl that's rich, wise, fair, and young;
The match (he saith) is half concluded, he
Indeed is wonderous willing; but not she.
And reason good, for he has run thro all
Almost the story of the Prodigal.
Yet swears he never with the hogs did dine
That's true, for none would trust him with their swine.

Some of our Sparks to London town go
Fashions to see, and learn the World to know;
Who at Return have naught but these to show,
New Wig above, and new Disease below.

Love, cough, and a smoke, can't be well hid.

Fine linen, girls and gold so bright
Chuse not to take by candle-light.

There are no ugly loves, nor handsome Prisons.

Women are Books, and men the Readers be,
Who sometimes in their books Erratas see;
Yet oft the Readers raptured with each line,
Fair print and paper frought with Sense divine;
Tho' some neglectful seldom care to read,
and faithful Wives no more than bibles heed.
Are Women books? Says Hodge,
Then would mine were an Almanack to change every year.

Prithee, isn't Miss Cloe's a comical case?
She lends out her Tail and she borrows her Face.

On His Late Deafness

Deaf, giddy, helpless, left alone,
To all my friends a Burthen grown,
No more I hear a great Church-Bell,
Than if it rang out for my knell:
At thunder now no more I start,
Than at the whispering of a F——t.
Nay, What's incredible alack!
I hardly hear my Bridget's Clack.

When Man and Woman die, as Poet's sung,
His hearts that last part that moves, her last, the tongue.

He is a Governor that governs his Passions,
and he a Servant that serves them.

Love and Be loved.

Nothing dries sooner than a tear.

The way to be safe, is never to be secure.
Dally not with other Folks' women or money.

She that paints her face
Thinks of her tail.

Poor Richard's Description of his Country Wife, Joan

A Song-Tune, The Hounds are all out.

Of their *Chloes* and *Phyllises* Poets may prate,
I will sing my plain country Joan;
Twice twelve years my wife, still the joy of my life,
Blessed day that I made her my own,
     My dear friends.
Blessed day that I made her my own.

Not a word of her shape, or her face, or her eyes,
Of flames or of darts shall you hear;
Though I beauty admire, 'tis Virtue I prize.
Which fades not in seventy years.

In health a companion delightful and gay,
Still easy engaging and free;
In sickness no less than the faithfullest nurse,
as tender as tender can be.

In peace and good order my Household she guides
Right careful to save what I gain;
Yet chearfully spends and smiles on the friends
I've the pleasure to entertain.

Am I laden with care, she takes off a share,
That the burden never makes me to reel;
Does good fortune arrive, the joy of my Wife
Quite doubles the pleasure I feel.

She defends my good name, even when I'm to blame
Friend firmer to man never was given.
Her compassionate breast feels for all the distressed,
which draws down the blessings of heaven.

In raptures the giddy rakes talks of his Fair,
Enjoyment will make him despise.
I speak my cool sense, with long experience
And acquaintance has changed in no wise.

The best have some faults, and so has MY JOAN,
But then they're exceedingly small.
And now I'm used to 'em, they're so like my own
I scarcely can feel them at all.

Was the fairest young princess, with millions in purse
To be had in exchange for MY JOAN
She could not be a better wife, might be a worse
So I'll stick to MY JUGGY alone.

MARRIAGE

A Catalogue of the Principal Kings and Princes in Europe, with the time of their births and Ages

George II King of Britain   Born 30 Oct. 1683   Age 50
Frederick Prince of Wales   Born 19 Jan. 1706   Age 27
Charles 6 Emporer of Germany   1 Oct. 1685   Age 48

Mary, Queen of France   23 June 1703   Age 30
Philip 5 King of Spain   19 Dec. 1683   Age 50
Frederick 4 King of Denmark   11 Oct. 1671   Age 62
Prince Eugene of Savoy   18 Oct. 1663   Age 70

Poor Richard an American Prince,
without Subjects, his wife being
Viceroy over him

                           23 Oct. 1684 Age 49

Little Half-wits are wonderous just we find,
Scoffing and jeering on whole Womankind
All False, All Whores, All this & that & t'other,
Not one exception left, ev'n for their Mother;
But men of Wisdom and Experience know

That there's no greater Happiness below
Than a good Wife affords, and such there's many
For every man has one, the best of any.

Three things are men most liable to be cheated in: a Horse, a
Wig, and a Wife.

Doris, a Widow, past her Prime,
Her Spouse long dead, her wailing doubles;
Her real griefs increase by Time,
What might abate, improves her troubles.
Those Pangs her prudent Hopes supprest,
Impatient now, she cannot smother,
How should the helpless woman rest?
One's gone, nor can she get another.

Keep your eyes wide open before marriage,
half shut afterwards.

Luke, on his dying bed, embrac'd his Wife,
And begg'd one Favour; Swear, my dearest Life,
Swear, if you love me, never more to wed,
Nor take a second husband to your Bed.
Anne dropt a tear. You know my dear says she,
Your least desires have still been Laws to me;
But from this Oath, I beg you'd me excuse;
For I'm already promis'd to J——n H——s.

[19]

You can bear your own Faults
and why not a fault in your Wife?

A Man without a Wife, is but half a Man.

Dick told his spouse, he durst behold to Swear
What'er she pray's for, Heav'n would thwart her.
Indeed! says Nell, 'tis what I'm pleas'd to hear,
For now I'll pray for your long life, my dear.

Marry above thy match and thou'lt get a Master.

Jane, why those tears? Why droops your head?
Is then your other husband dead?
Or doth a worse disgrace betide?
Hath no one since his death apply'd?

Epitaph on a Scolding Wife by her Husband

Here my poor Bridget's Corps doth lie, she is at rest
——and so am I.

Marry your son when you will
but your daughter when you can.

When there's Marriage without love,
There will be Love without marriage.

1735

Courteous Reader,

This is the third time of my appearing in print, hitherto very much to my own satisfaction, and, I have reason to hope, to the satisfaction of the publick also; for the publick is generous, and has been charitable and good to me. I should be ungrateful, then, if I did not take every opportunity of expressing my gratitude; I therefore return the publick my most humble and hearty thanks.

Whatever may be the music of the spheres, how great soever the harmony of the stars, 'tis certain there is no harmony among the stargazers; but they are perpetually growling and snarling at one another like strange curs, or like some men at their wives: I had resolved to keep the peace on my own part, and affront none of them; and I shall persist in that resolution; but having received much abuse from Titan Leeds deceased (Titan Leeds when living would not have used me so) I say, having received much abuse from the ghost of Titan Leeds, who pretends to be still living, and to write Almanacks in spite of me and my predictions, I cannot help saying, that though I take it patiently, I take it very unkindly. And whatever he may pretend, 'tis undoubtedly true that he is really defunct and dead. First because the stars are seldom disappointed, and they foreshowed his death at the time I predicted it. Secondly, 'tis requisite and necessary he should die punctually at that time, for the honor of astrology, the art professed both by him and his father before him. Thirdly, 'tis plain to everyone that reads his last two Almanacks (for 1734 and 35) that they are not written with that *life* his performances used to be written with; the wit is low and flat, the little hints dull and spiritless, nothing smart in them but Hubidra's verses against Astrology at the heads of the months in the last, which no astrologer but a *dead* one would have inserted, and no man *living* would or could write such stuff as the rest. But lastly, I shall convince him from his own words that he is dead, for in the preface to his almanack for 1734 he says, "Saunders adds another gross falsehood in his Almanack, *viz.* that by my own calculation I shall survive until the 26th of the said month October 1733, which is as untrue as the former." Now if it be, as Leeds says, "untrue" and a "gross falsehood" that he survived till the 26th of October 1733, then it is certainly *true* that he died *before* that time. And if he died before that time, he is dead now, to all intents and purposes, anything he may say to the contrary notwithstanding. And at what time before the 26th it is so likely he should die, as at the time by me predicted, *viz.*, the 17th of October aforesaid? But if some people will walk and be troublesome after death, it may perhaps be borne with a little, because it cannot well be avoided unless one would be at the pains and expense of laying them in the Red Sea; however, they should not presume too much upon the liberty allowed them. I know confinement must needs be mighty irksome to the free spirit of an astronomer, and I am too compassionate to proceed suddenly to extremities with it; I shall not long defer, if it does not speedily learn to treat its living friends with better manners. I am,

Courteous Readers,
Your obliged friend and servant,

October 30, 1735.   R. SAUNDERS

RELIGION

Epitaph on a Worthy Clergyman

Still like his Master, known by breaking bread,
The good he entertain'd, the needy fed;
Of humor easy, and of life unblam'd,
The friend delighted, while the priest see laim'd.
The friend, the father, and the husband gone,
The priest still lives in this recording stone;
Where pious eyes may read his praises o'er,
and learn each grace his pulpit taught before.

❈

Epitaph on another Clergyman

Here lies, who need not here be nam'd,
For theologic knowledge fam'd;
Who all the bible had by rote,
With all the comments Calvin wrote;
Parsons and Jesuits could confute,
Talk infidels and Quakers mute,
To every heretic a foe;
Was he an honest man—?
so so.

Many have quarreled about Religion
That never practised it.

Danger is sauce for prayers.

POLITICS

Kings and Bears often worry their keepers.

The greatest monarch on the proudest throne
is oblig'd to sit upon his own arse.

He that can take rest
is greater than he that can take cities.

Robbers must exalted be,
Small ones on the Gallow-Tree,
While greater ones ascend to thrones,
But what is that to thee or me?

Ye Party Zealots, thus it fares with you,
When party rage too warmly you persue;
Both sides club nonsense and impetuous pride,
And folly joins whom sentiments divide.
You vent your spleen as monkeys when they pass,
Scratch at the mimic monkey in the glass,

While both are one; and henceforth be it known,
Fools of both sides shall stand as fools alone.

In rivers and bad Governments
The lightest things swim at top.

Many princes sin with David
but few repent with him.

You may give a man an Office
but you cannot give him discretion.

Where there is hunger, law is not regarded
and where law is not regarded there will be hunger.

Laws too gentle are seldom obeyed,
too severe, seldom executed.

1736

Loving Readers,

Your kind acceptance of my former labors has encouraged me to continue writing, though the general approbation you have been so good as to favour me with, has excited the envy of some, and drawn upon me the malice of others. These ill-willers of mine, despited at the great reputation I gained by exactly predicting another man's death, have endeavored to deprive me of it all at once, in the most effectual manner, by reporting that I myself was never alive. They say in short that there is no such man as I am, and have spread this notion so thoroughly in the country, that I have frequently been told it to my face by those that don't know me. This is not civil treatment, to endeavor to deprive me of my very being, and reduce me to a non-entity in the opinion of the publick. But so long as I know myself to walk about, eat, drink and sleep, I am satisfied that *there is really such a man as I am*, whatever they may say to the contrary: And the world may be satisfied likewise; for if there were no such man as I am, how is it possible I should appear publickly to hundreds of people, as I have done for several years past in print? I need not, indeed, have taken any notice of so idle a report, if it had not been for the sake of my printer, to whom my enemies are pleased to ascribe my productions, and who it seems is as unwilling to father my offspring as I am to lose the credit of it. Therefore to clear him entirely, as well as to vindicate my own honor, I make this publick and serious declaration, which I desire may be believed, to wit, *That what I have written heretofore, and do now write, neither was nor is written by another man or men, person or persons whatever*. Those who are not satisfied with this, must needs be very unreasonable.

My performance for this year follows; it submits itself, kind reader, to thy censure, but hopes for thy candor, to forgive its faults. It devotes itself entirely to thy Service, and will serve thee faithfully. And if it has the good fortune to please its master, 'tis gratification enough for the labour of

Poor

R. SAUNDERS.

MONEY & BUSINESS

Light purse, heavy heart.

The poor have little, beggars none,
the rich too much, enough not one.

The old man has given all to his son; O fool!
To undress thy self before thou art going to bed.

He does not possess Wealth, it possesses him.

Wealth is not his that has it, but his that enjoys it.

I'm prudent Jack, who now lives by his Shifts,
Borrowing of Driblets, boldly begging gifts;
For twenty shillings lent him t'other day
(By one who ne'er expected he would pay)

On his friend's paper fain a Note would write;
His friend, as needless, did refuse it quite;
Paper was scarce, and 'twas too hard, it's true,
To part with cash and loose his paper too.

Can Wealth give happiness? Look round and see,
What gay distress! What splendid Misery!

When the young Trader, aided by your loan,
Thrives in his trade, a worthy merchant grown;
When, snatched from ruin's jaws by your kind hand,
The farmer pays his debts and saves his land;
When good like this is done, your money lent
Brings you, beside your Interest, cent. per cent.
In pleasing satisfaction and content.

Many a man would have been worse
if his Estate had been better.

Lend money to an enemy, and thou'lt gain him,
to a friend and thou'lt lose him.

Beware of little Expences,
a small leak will sink a great ship.

Can Gold calm Passion, or make Reason shine,
Can we dig peace, or wisdom from the Mine?
Wisdom to gold prefer, than our happiness.
That happiness with Great ones often see,
With rage and wonder, in a low degree,
Themselves unblest. The Poor are only poor;
But what are they who droop amid their store?

When prosperity was well mounted,
she let go the Bridle,
and soon came tumbling out of the saddle.

There are three faithful friends—
An old wife, an old dog,
and ready money.

Fools need Advice the most
but wise men only
are the better for it.

Learn of the skillful:
He that teaches himself
hath a fool for a master.

He that is of the opinion money will do everything
may well be suspected of doing everything for money.

Drive thy Business! Let not it drive you.

Bargaining has neither friends nor relations.

⚘

Gifts burst rocks.

How to Get RICHES

The art of getting Riches consists
very much in Thrift. All men are not equally
qualified for getting money, but it is in the power
of every one alike to practise this virtue.
He that would be beforehand in the
World, must be beforehand with his business:
It is not only ill Management, but discovers a slothful
Disposition, to do that in the afternoon,
which should be done in the morning.
Useful attainments in your minority
will procure riches in maturity, of which
Writing and accounts are not of the moment.

Precept I

In things of moment, on thy self depend,
Nor trust too far thy servant or thy friend:
With private views, thy friend may promise fair,
And servants very seldom prove sincere.

Precept II

What can be done, with care perform today,
Dangers unthought of will attend delay;
Your distant prospects, all precarious are,
And fortune is as fickle as she's fair.

Precept III

Nor trivial loss, nor trivial gain despise;
Molehills, if often heaped, to Mountains rise:
Weigh every small Expence, and nothing waste,
Farthings long sav'd, amount to Pounds at last.

Discontented minds, and fevers of the body,
are not to be changed by changing beds or businesses.

He that builds before he counts the cost,
acts foolishly;
and he that counts before he builds,
finds he did not count wisely.

The Busy-Man's Picture

Business, thou plague and Pleasure of my life,
Thou charming mistress, thou vextious Wife;
Thou enemy, thou friend, to Joy, to Grief,
Thou bring'st me all, and bring'st me no relief,
Thou bitter, sweet, thou pleasing, teazing thing,
Thou bee, that with thy honey wears a sting;
Some respite, prithee do, yet do not give,
I cannot with thee, nor without thee live.

Neccessity never made a good bargain.

He that riseth late must trot all day
and shall scarce overtake his business at night.

'Tis against some men's principle to pay interest
and seems against others' interest
to pay the principal.

Patience in market is worth pounds in a year.

1737

————◆◆————

Courteous and kind Reader,

This is the fifth time I have appeared in public, chalking out the future year for my honest Countrymen, and foretelling what shall and what may come to pass; in which I have the pleasure to find that I have given general satisfaction. Indeed, among the multitude of our astrological predictions, 'tis no wonder if some few fail, for without any defect in the art itself, 'tis well known that a small error, a single wrong figure overseen in a calculation, may occasion great mistakes. But however we Almanack-makers may miss it in other things, I believe it will generally be allowed that we always hit the day of the month and that I suppose is esteemed one of the most useful things in an Almanack.

As to the weather, if I were to fall into the method of my brother, J——n, sometimes uses, and tell you "Snow here in New England ... Rain here or in South Carolina ... cold to the northward ... warm to the southward," and the like, whatever errors I might commit, I should be something more secure of not being detected in them. But I consider, it will be of no service to know what weather it is 1,000 miles off, and therefore I always set down positively what weather my reader will have, be he where he will at that time. We modestly desire only the favorable allowance of a day or two before and a day or two after the precise day against which the weather is set, and if it does not come to pass accordingly, let the fault be laid upon the printer who, 'tis very like, may have transposed or misplaced it, perhaps for the convieniency of putting in his hollidays, and since, in spite of all I can say, people will give him great part of the credit of

[42]

making my Almanacks, 'tis but reasonable he should take some share of the blame.

I must not omit here to thank the publick for the gracious and kind encouragement they have hitherto given me: but if the generous purchaser of my labours could see how often his six-pence helps to light up the comfortable fire, line the pot, fill the cup and make glad the heart of a poor man and an honest good old woman, he would not think his money ill laid out, tho' the Almanack of his

Friend and Servant

R. Saunders

were one half blank paper.

FOOLS

The World is full of fools and faint hearts, and yet every one has courage enough to bear the misfortunes and wisdom enough to manage the affairs of his neighbour.

Who knows a fool, must know his brother
For one will recommend another.

He's a Fool that cannot conceal his Wisdom

Fools make feasts and wise men eat them.

A Flatterer never seems absurd:
The Flatter'd always take his word.

The heart of a fool is in his mouth, but the mouth of a wise man is in his heart.

A learned blockhead is a greater blockhead than an ignorant one.

The most exquisite Folly is made of Wisdom spun too fine.

If your head is wax
don't walk in the sun.

The wise man draws more
Advantage from his enemies
than the Fool from his friends.

The first Degree of Folly is to conceit one's self wise;
the second to profess it;
the third to despise Counsel.

The learned Fool writes his Nonsense
in better Languages
than the unlearned;
but still it's nonsense.

Experience keeps a dear school, but fools will
learn in no other
And scarce in that.

It is Ill-Manners to silence a Fool
and cruelty to let him go on.

Blame-all and Praise-all are two blockheads.

Monkeys warm with envious spite
their most obliging friends will bite;
And, fond to copy human ways,
Practise new mischiefs all their days.

Tricks and treachery are the practise of fools
that have not wit enough to be honest.

Once on a time it by chance came to pass,
That a man and his son were leading an ass.
Cries a passenger, neighbour, you're shrewdly put to't,
to lead an ass empty, and trudge it on foot.
Nay, quoth the old fellow, if folk do so mind us
I'll e'en climb the ass, and boy mount behind us.
But as they jogg'd on, they were laughed at and hissed,

What, two booby Lubbers on one sorry beast!
This is such a figure as never was known;
'Tis is a sign that the ass is none of your own.
Then down gets the boy, and walks by the side,
Till another cries, what, you old fool, must you ride?
When you see the poor child that weakly and young
Forc'd thro' thick and thin to trudge it along.
Then down gets the father and up gets the son;
If this cannot please them we ne'er shall have done,
they had not gone far, but a woman cries out,
O you young graceless Imp, you'll be hang'd no doubt!
Must you ride an ass, and your father that's gray
Foot it, and pick out the best of his way?
So now to please all they but one trick lack,
and that was to carry the ass a pick-pack.:
But when that was try'd, it appear'd such a jest,
It occasioned more laughter by half than the rest.
Thus he who'd please all, and their good-liking gain
Shows a deal good-nature, but labours in vain.

PRIDE & HUMILITY

Whate'er's desired, knowledge, Fame, or Pelf,
Not one will change his neighbour with himself.
The learn'd are happy Nature to explore,
The Fool is happy that he knows no more.
The Rich are happy in the Plenty given;
The Poor contents him with the *Care of Heav'n*.
Thus does some comfort ev'ry State attend,
And Pride's bestow'd on all, a common friend.

He that falls in love with himself,
will have no rivals.

He that cannot bear with other People's Passions
cannot govern his own.

Pride is as loud a Beggar as Want
and a great deal more saucy.

The Proud hate Pride—in others.

Pride dines upon Vanity, sups on Contempt.

Great Pride and Meanness sure are near ally'd,
Or thin Particulars do their Bounds divide.

To be *proud* of knowledge, is to be *blind* with Light;
to be *proud* of virtue is to poison yourself with
the Antidote

Pride breakfasted with Plenty
Dined with poverty
supped with Infamy.

Men meet, mountains never.

Quarrels never could last long
If one side only lay the wrong.

Self Love but serves the virtuous Mind to Wake,
As the small Pebble stirs the peaceful Lake;
The Centre mov'd, a circle strait succeeds,
Another still, and still another spreads,

[53]

Friend, Parent, Neighbour, first it will embrace,
His country next, and next all human Race.
Wide and more wide, th' o'erflowings of the Mind
Take every Creature in of every kind.

Declaiming against Pride is not
Always a sign of Humility.

In success be moderate.

Humility makes great men twice honourable.

Blessed is he that expects nothing
for he shall never be disappointed.

Success has ruined many a man.

The Reverse

Studious of Ease, and fond of humble things,
Below the Smiles, below the frowns of Kings,
Thanks to my stars, I prize the sweets of life,
No sleepless nights I count, no days of Strife.

I rest, I wake, I drink, I sometimes love,
I read, I write, I settle or I rove;
Content to live, content to die unknown,
Lord of myself, accountable to none.

To be humble to Superiors is Duty,
to equals courtesy,
to inferiors nobleness.

After crosses and losses
Men grow humbler and wiser.

1738

PREFACE by Mrs. Saunders

Dear Readers,

My good man set out last week for Potowmack, to visit an old stargazer of his acquaintance, and see about a little place for us to settle and end our days on. He left the copy of his Almanack sealed up, and bid me send it to the press. I suspected something, and therefore as soon as he was gone, I opened it, to see if he had not been flinging some of his old Skitts at me. Just as I thought, so he was. And truly (for want of something else to say I suppose) he had put into his preface that his wife Bridget was this and that and t'other. What a peasecods! Cannot I have a little fault or two, but all the country must see it in print! They have already been told, at one time that I am proud, another time that I am loud, and that I have got a new petticoat, and abundance of such kind of stuff; and now, forsooth! all the world must know that poor *Dick's* wife has lately taken a fancy to drink a little tea now and then. A mighty matter, truly, to make a song of! 'Tis true, I had a little tea of a present from the printer last year, and what, must a body throw it away? In short, I thought the Preface was not worth a printing and so I fairly scratched it all out, and I believe you'll like our Almanack never the worse for it.

Upon looking over the months, I see he has put in an abundance of foul weather this year, and therefore I 'have scattered here and there, where I could find room, some *fair pleasant sunshiny,* & C. for the good-women to dry their clothes in. If it does not come to pass according to my desire, I have shown my good-will, however, and I hope they'll take it in good part.

I had a design to make some other corrections and particularly to change some of the verses that I don't very well like, but I have just now unluckily broke my spectacles which obliges me to give it you as it is, and conclude,

Your loving Friend

Bridget Saunders.

DRINKING & EATING

Eat to live and not live to eat.

He that drinks fast, pays slow.

Never mind it, she'll be sober after the Holidays.

What Death is, dost Thou ask of me;
Till dead I do not know;
Come to me when thou hear'st I'm dead;
Then what 'tis I shall show.
To die's to cease to be, it seems,
So learned Seneca did think;
But we've Philosophers of modern Date
Who say 'tis Death to cease to Drink.

Some have learnt Tricks of sly Evasion,
Instead of Truth they use Equivocation,
And eke it out with mental Reservation,

Which to good Men is an Abomination.
Our Smith of late most wonderfully swore,
That whilst he breathed he would drink no more;
But since, I know his meaning, for I think
He meant he would not breath whilst he did drink.

Drink does not drown Care, but waters it,
and makes it grow fast.

He that spills the Rum, loses that only; He
that drinks it, often loses both that and himself.

Three good meals a day is bad living.

TALKING

Keep your mouth wet, feet dry.

Here comes the Orator! With his flood of words,
and his Drop of Reason.

He that speaks much, is much mistaken.

Well done is better than well said.

The worst wheel of the cart
makes the most noise.

Great talkers should be cropt
for they've no need of ears.

Epitaph on a Talkative Maid

Beneath this silent Stone is laid,
A Noisy antiquated Maid,
Who from her Craddle talk'd 'till Death,
And ne'er before was out of Breath.
Whither she's gone we cannot tell;
For, if she talks not, she's in Hell:
If she's in Heaven, she's there unblest,
Because she hates a Place of Rest.

Proclaim not all thou knowest, all thou owest,
all thou hast, nor all thou canst.

Words may shew a man's Wit, but
Actions his meaning.

A great Talker may be no Fool,
but he is one that relies on him.

1740

Courteous Reader,

You may remember that in my first Almanack, published for the year 1733, I predicted the death of my dear friend Titan Leeds to happen that year on the 17th day of October 3h. 29m. P.M. The good man, it seems, died accordingly, but W.B. and A.B. continue to publish almanacks in his name ever since, asserting for some years that he was still living. At length, when the truth could no longer be concealed from the world, they confess his death in their Almanack for 1739, but pretend that he died not till last year, and that before his departure he had furnished them with calculations for 7 years to come. Ah, my friends, these are poor shifts and thin disguises, of which indeed I should have taken little or no notice, if you had not at the same time accused me as a false predictor, an aspersion that the more affects me, as my whole livelihood depends on a contrary character.

But to put this whole matter beyond dispute, I shall acquaint the world with a fact, as strange and surprising as it is true, being as follows, *viz.*

On the 4th Instant, towards midnight, as I sat in my little study writing this Preface, I fell fast asleep, and continued in that condition for some time, without dreaming anything, to my knowledge. On awaking, I found lying before me the following letter, *viz.*

Dear Friend Saunders,

My respect for you continues even in this separate state, and I am grieved to see the aspersions thrown on you by the malevolence of avaricious publishers of Almanacks who envy your success. They say your prediction of my death in 1733 was false and they pretend that I remained alive many years after. But I do hereby certify that I did actually die at that time, precisely at that time you mentioned with a variation only of 5 min. 53 sec. which must be allowed to be no great matter in such cases. And I do further declare that I furnished them with no calculations of the planets' motion, etc., seven years after my death as they are pleased to give out, so that the stuff they publish as an almanack in my name is no more mine than 'tis yours.

You will wonder, perhaps, how this paper comes written on your table. You must know that no separate spirits are under any confinement till after the final settlement of all accounts. In the meantime we wander where we please, visit our old friends, observe their actions, enter sometimes into their imaginations, and give them hints waking or sleeping that may be of advantage to them. Finding you asleep, I entered your left nostril, ascended into your brain, found out where the ends of those nerves were fastened that moved your right hand and fingers by the help of which I am now writing unknown to you; but when you open your eyes, you will see that the handwriting is mine, though wrote with yours.

The people of this infidel age, perhaps, will hardly believe this story. But you may give them these three signs by which they shall be convinced of the truth of it. About the middle of June Philomat shall be openly reconciled to the Church of Rome, and give all his goods and Chattles to the Chappel, being perverted by a certain Country School Master. On the 7th of September following, my old friend W.B. shall be sober 9 hours, to the astonishment of his neighbours. And about the same time W.B. and A.B. will publish another Almanack in my name, in spite of truth and common sense.

As I can see much clearer into futurity, since I got free from the dark prison of Self, in which I was continually molested and almost blinded with fogs, I shall in kindness to you frequently give you

information of things to come, for the improvement of your Almanack. Being Dear Dick
  Your affectionate Friend,

T. LEEDS

For my own part I am convinced that the above letter is genuine. If the reader doubts of it, let him carefully observe the three signs; and if they do not actually come to pass, believe as he pleases.

  I am his humble Friend,

R. SAUNDERS

VIRTUE

Relationship without friendship, friendship
without power, power without will, will
without effect, effect without profit,
profit without virtue,
are not worth a farto.

He that lies down with dogs,
shall rise up with fleas.

All things are easy to Industry,
All things are difficult to sloth.

Take this remark from Richard poor and lame,
Whate'er's begun in anger ends in shame.

Be slow in chusing a friend,
slower in changing.

Early to bed and early to rise
Makes a man healthy, wealthy, and wise.

The Sun never repents of the good he does,
nor does he ever demand recompense.

If what most men admire, they would despise,
'Twould look as if mankind were growing wise.

Don't throw stones at your neighbours
if your own windows are glass.

The excellency of hogs is fatness, of men virtue.

He that would live in peace and not ease
Must not speak all he knows
Nor judge all he sees.

The nearest way to come at glory,
is to do that for conscience
which we do for glory.

To morrow you'll reform, you always cry;
In what far country does this morrow lie,
That 'tis so mighty long e'er it arrive?
Beyond the Indies does this morrow live?
'Tis so far-fetch'd, this morrow, that I fear,
'Twill be be both very old, and very dear.
To morrow I'll reform, the Fool does say:
Today it self's too late; the Wise did yesterday.

The noblest question in the world is
What good may I do in it?

Sell not virtue to purchase wealth
nor liberty to purchase power.

Hast thou Virtue?
Acquire also the graces and beauties of virtue.

Nothing brings more pain than too much pleasure;
nothing more bondage than too much liberty.

Let thy vices die before thee.

Search others for their virtues, thy self for thy vices.

Wink at small faults;
remember thou hast great ones.

Each year one vicious habit rooted out,
In time might make the worst man
good throughout.

There is much difference between imitating
a good man
and counterfeiting him.

Defer not thy well-doing;
be not like St. George,
who is always a horseback, and never rides on.

Honour thy Father and Mother,
Live so as to be
an Honour to them tho' they are dead.

Hear no ill of a friend,
nor speak any of an enemy.

A good example is the best sermon.

Strive to be the greatest man in your county
and you may be disappointed;
Strive to be the best and you may succeed:
He may well win the race who runs by himself.

To make the cleanly kitchen send up food,
Not costly vain, but plentifully good,
To bid the cellars fountain never fail
Of sparkling cyder, or of well-brew'd Ale;
To buy, to pay, to blame, or to approve,
Within, without, below-stairs, and above;
To shine in every corner, like the sun,
Still working everywhere, or looking on.

An Hour sometimes in Hospitals employ,
To give the dying wretch a glimpse of joy;
T'attend the crowds that hopeless Pangs endure,
And soothe the Anguish which they cannot cure;
To clothe the bare, and give the Empty food;
As bright as guardian angels, and as good.

Pardoning the bad is injuring the good.

He is not well-bred
that cannot bear ill-breeding in others.

Having been poor is no shame;
but being ashamed of it is.

Many a man thinks he is buying pleasure
When he is really selling himself
a slave to it.

'Tis hard but glorious to be poor and honest.

Content let all your Virtues lie unknown,
If there's no tongue to praise them but your own
Of boasting more than of a bomb afraid,
Merit should be as modest as a Maid.

'Tis a shame that your family is an honour to you!
You ought to be an honour to your family.

Who rise to glory must by Virtue rise,
'Tis in the mind all genuine greatness lies.
On that eternal base, on that alone,
The world's esteem you build, and more—your own.
For what avails Birth, Beauty, Fortune's store,
The plume of title, and the pride of Pow'r,
If, deaf to virtue, deaf to honour's call,
To tyrant Vice a wretched slave you fall?

The busy man has few idle visitors;
to the boiling pot the flies come not.

Meanness is the parent of insolence.

If you would reap Praise you must sow the seeds,
Gentle words and useful deeds.

Anger is never without a reason
but seldom with a good one.

Virtue and a trade are a child's best portion.

Love thy neighbour,
Yet don't pull down your hedge.

He that doth what he should not,
Shall feel what he would not.

The honest man takes pains
and then enjoys pleasures;
The knave takes pleasures and then suffers pains.

Think of three things:
Whence you came,
where you are going,
and to whom you must account.

Bad gains are truly losses.

Neglect mending a small fault
and 'twill soon be a great one.

Being ignorant is not so much a shame
as being unwilling to learn.

Love your enemies
For they tell you your faults.

Be civil to all,
serviceable to many,
familiar with few,
Friend to one,
Enemy to none.

Tell me my faults and mend your own.

Work as if you were to live 100 years,
Pray as if you were to die tomorrow.

Good sense and learning may esteem obtain,
Humorous and wit a laugh, if rightly ta'en;
Fair virtue Admiration may impart:
But 'tis good-nature only wins the heart.
It moulds the body to an easy grace,
And brightens every feature of the face;
It smooths th'unpolish'd tongue with eloquence
and adds persuasion to the finest sense.

Be always ashamed to catch thyself idle.

Let thy discontents be thy secrets;
if the world knows them,
'twill despise thee and increase them.

Fear to do ill, and you need fear nought else.

Observe all men,
thy self most.

The things which hurt, instruct.

What you would seem to be, be really.

Who is strong?
He that can conquer his bad habits.
Who is rich?
He that rejoices in his portion.

Cut the wings of your desires and hopes
lest they lead you a weary dance after them.

Praise little, dispraise less.

Some make conscience of wearing a hat in the church
who make none of robbing the altar.

Trouble springs from idleness,
toil from ease.

Laziness travels so slowly that poverty soon
overtakes it.

Half the truth is often a great lie.

In other men we faults can spy
And blame the mote that dims their eye;
Each little speck and blemish find
To our own stronger errors blind.

1746

PREFACE

Who is Poor Richard? People oft enquire,
Where lives? What is he? ——never yet the
Somewhat to ease your curiosity   (nigher
Take these slight sketches of my dame and me.
Thanks to kind readers and a careful wife,
With plenty blessed, I lead an easy life;
My business writing; her's to drain the Mead,
or crown the barren hill with useful shade;
In the smooth Gleb to see the plowshare worn,
And fill the granary with needful corn.
Press nectarous cyder from my loaded trees,
Print the sweet butter, turn the drying cheese.
Some books we read, though few there are that hit
The happy point where wisdom joins with wit;
That set fair virtue naked to our view,
And teach us what is decent, what is true.
The friend sincere, and honest man, with joy
Treating or treated oft our time employ.
Our table neat, meal temperate, and our door
Opening spontaneous to the bashful poor.
Free from the bitter rage of party zeal,
All those we love who seek the publick weal.
Now blindly follow superstitions lore,
Which cheats deluded mankind over and over.
Not over righteous, quite beyond the rule,

Conscience perplext by every canting tool.
Nor yet when folly hides the dubious line,
Where good and bad their blended colors join;
Rush indiscreetly down the dangerous steep,
And plunge uncertain in the darksome deep.
Cautious, if right; if wrong resolved to part
The inmate snake that folds about the heart.
Observe the mean, the motive and the end;
Mending ourselves, or striving still to mend.
Our souls sincere, our purpose fair and free,
Without vain glory or hypocrisy;
Thankful if well; if ill, we kiss the rod,
Resign with hope, and put our trust in God.

MORTALITY

Each Age of men new fashions doth invent;
Things which are old, young Men do not esteem:
What pleas'd our fathers, doth not us content;
What flourish'd then, we out of fashion deem:
And that's the reason, as I understand,
Why Prodigus did sell his Father's land.

Death is a Fisherman, the world we see
His Fish-pond is, and we the Fishes be:
His net some general sickness; howe'er he
Is not so kind as other Fishers be;
For if they take one of the smaller fry,
They throw him in again, he shall not die:
But Death is sure to kill all he can get,
And all is Fish with him that comes to Net.

By nought is Man from beast distinguished
More than by knowledge in his learned head.
Then Youth improves thy Time, but cautious see
That what thou learnest some how useful be.
Each day improving, Salon waxed old;
For time he knew was better far than Gold.

Fortune might give him Gold which would decay,
but Fortune cannot give him Yesterday.

If you would not be forgotten
As soon as you are dead and rotten,
Either write things worth reading
or do things worth writing.

Since thou art not sure of a minute,
throw not away an hour.

Wish not so much to live long as to live well.

When Death put out our Flame
the Snuff will tell
If we were wax, or tallow by the smell.

Lord, if our days be few, why do we spend
And lavish them to such an Evil End?
Or why, if they be evil, do we wrong
Our selves and Thee, in wishing them so long?
Our Days decrease, our evils still renew,
We make them ill,
Thou kindly mak'st them few.

Think, bright Florella, when you see
The constant Changes of the Year,
That nothing is from Ruin free,
And gayest things must disappear.
Think of your beauties in their bloom,
The Spring of sprightly Youth improve;
For cruel Age, alas, will come
And then 'twill be too late to love.

In Travel, Pilgrims oft do ask to know
What miles they've gone, and what they have to go;
Their way is tedious and their limbs opprest,
And their desire is to be at rest.
In life's more tedious Journey, Man delays
T'enquire out the number of his Days:
He cares, not he, how slow his hours spend,
The Journey's better than the Journey's end.

In Travel, Pilgrims oft do ask to know

Old Age will come, Disease may come before,
Fifteen is full as mortal as Threescore.
Thy Fortune and thy Charms may soon decay;
But grant these fugitives prolong their stay:
Their basis totters, their foundation shakes,
Life that supports them, in a moment breaks:
Then, wrought into the soul, let Virtue shine,
The Ground eternal, as the Work divine.

All would live long
but none would be old.

Youth is pert and positive,
Age modest and doubting;
So ears of corn when young and light
stand bold upright,
But hang their heads when weighty, full, and ripe.

Ah! What is life? With ills encompassed round,
Amidst our hopes, Fate strikes the sudden wound,
Today the Statesman of new honour dreams,
Tomorrow death destroys his airy schemes.
Is mouldy treasures in thy chest confin'd,
Think, all that treasure thou must leave behind;
Thy heir with smiles shall view thy blazon'd hearse,
And all thy hoards, with lavish hand disperse.

For age and want save while you may;
No morning sun lasts a whole day.

Do not squander time,
For that's what life is made of.

Enjoy the present hour, be mindful of the past,
And neither fear nor wish the Approaches
of the past.

What's beauty? Call ye that your own,
A Flow'r that fades as soon as blown!
Those eyes of so divine a ray,
What are they? Mould'ring mortal clay.
Those features cast in heav'nly mould,
Shall like my coarser Earth, grow old,
Like common grass, the fairest Flou'r
Must feel the hoary Season's pow'r.

Syl dreamt that bury'd in his fellow clay,
Close by a common Beggar's side he lay:
And, as so mean a neighbour shock'd his pride
Thus, like a corpse of consequence, he cry'd:
Scoundrel, begone; and henceforth touch me not:
More manners learn; and, at a distance, rot.
How! Scoundrel! in a haughtier Tone cry'd he;
Proud lump of dirt, I scorn thy words and thee,
Here all are equal, now thy case is mine,
This is my rotting place, and that is thine.

Kings have long arms, but Misfortune longer,
Let none think themselves out of her Reach.

You may delay, but time will not;
Lost time is never seen again.

❀

Ah simple man!
When a boy two precious jewels were given thee,
Time and good advice,
one thou has lost
and the other thrown away.

1747

Courteous Reader,

This is the 15th time I have entertained thee with my annual productions, I hope to thy profit as well as mine. For besides the astronomical calculations, and other things usually contained in almanacks, which have their daily use indeed while the year continues, but then become of no value, I have constantly interspersed moral sentences, prudent maxims, and wise sayings, many of them containing much good sense in very few words, and therefore apt to leave strong and lasting impressions on the memory of young persons, whereby they may receive benefit as long as they live, when both Almanack and Almanack-maker have been long thrown by and forgotten. If I now or then insert a joke or two, that seem to have little in them, my apology is that such may have their use, since perhaps for their sake light and airy minds peruse the rest, and so are struck by somewhat of more weight and moment. The verses on the heads of the months are also generally designed to have the same tendency. I need not tell thee that not many of them are of my own making. If thou has any judgment in poetry, thou wilt easily discern the workman from the bungler. I know as well as thee that I am no poet born, and it is a trade I never learnt, nor indeed could learn. If I make verses 'tis in spight of nature and my stars I write. Why then should I give my readers bad lines of my own, when good ones of other people are of plenty? 'Tis methinks a poor excuse for the bad entertainment of guests, that the food we set before them, though coarse and ordinary, is of one's own raising, of one's own plantation, and when there is plenty of what is ten times better to be had in the market—on the contrary I assure ye, my friends, that I have procured the best I could for ye, and much good may it do ye.

I am thy poor friend to serve thee,

R. Saunders

A MISCELLANY

Visits should be short, like a winter's day,
Lest you're too troublesome hasten away.

Hunger never saw bad bread.

Beware of meat twice boil'd.
And of an old foe reconcil'd.

Snow winter, a plentiful harvest.

Fish and visitors stink in three days.

He that lives upon hope, dies farting.

Admiration is the daughter of Ignorance.

The tongue was once a servant to the heart,
And what it gave she freely did impart;
But now hypocrisy is grown so strong
The heart's become a servant to the tongue.
(Athenian-like), we act not what we know
As many men do talk of Robin Hood
Who never did shoot arrow in his bow.

None preaches better than the ant,
and she says nothing.

He that composes himself
is wiser than he that composes books.

I never saw an oft-transplanted tree,
nor yet an oft-removed family,
That throve so well as those
that settled be.

Who has deceiv'd thee as oft as thy self?

Write with the learned,
Pronounce with the vulgar.

None but the well-bred man knows
how to confess a fault
or acknowledge himself in an error.

Trust thy self
and another shall not betray thee.

Let thy discontents be secrets.

Beware of him that is slow to anger:
He is angry for something, and will not be pleased for nothing.

Great beauty, great strength and great riches
are really and truly of no great use;
a right heart exceeds all.

A true great man will neither trample on a worm
nor sneak to an emperor.

He that won't be counsell'd, can't be help'd.

Write injuries in dust, benefits in marble.

He that's secure is not safe.

Suspicion may be no great fault,
but showing it may be a great one.

Muse, shoes; days, stays; serene, between;
Air, fair; Life, wife, strife, etc., etc.
Rhimes, you see, are plenty enow; he
that does not like blank verse, may
add them at his leisure, as the
poets do at Manhattan.

It was wise council given to a young man,
Pitch upon that course of life which is most
excellent, and custom will make it the most
delightful. But many pitch on no course of life at all,
nor form any scheme of living, by which to attain any
valuable end; but wander perpetually from one
thing to another.

There are three things extreamly hard,
steel, a diamond, and to know one's self.

Woulds't thou confound thy enemy,
be good thy self.

Let thy servant be strong, faithful, and homely.

You may be too cunning for one but not for all.

Hide not your talents, they for use were made.
What's a sun dial in the shade?

What signifies knowing the names
if you know not the natures of things?

Glass, China, and Reputation
are easily cracked
and never well mended.

Most people return small favours,
acknowledge middling ones,
and repay great ones with ingratitude.

Don't judge of men's wealth or piety
by their Sunday appearances.

Friendship's increased by visiting friends,
But by visiting seldom.

A brother may not be a friend
but a friend will always be a brother.

Mankind are very odd creatures;
one half censure that they practise,
the other half practise what they censure,
the rest always say and do as they ought.

If a man could have half his wishes,
he would double his troubles.

He that best understands the world, least likes it.

When out of favour, none know thee;
when in, thou dost not know thyself.

Sudden power is apt to be insolent,
sudden liberty saucy,
that balances best which has grown gradually.

The discontented man finds no easy chair.

Take heed of the vinegar of sweet wine
and the anger of good-nature.

The horse thinks one thing
and he that saddles him another.

Little rogues easily become great ones.

Where sense is wanting
everything is wanting.

The wolf sheds his coat once a year,
his disposition never.

There was never a good knife made of bad steel.

Who is wise?
He that learns from everyone.
He that governs his passions.
He that is content.
Nobody.

The doors of wisdom are never shut.

The Master's eye will do more work than both his hands.

A change of fortune hurts a wise man
no more than a change of the moon.

Vain-glory flowereth but beareth no fruit.

A wise man will desire no more than what
he may get justly,
use soberly, distribute chearfully,
and leave contentedly.

A fake friend and a shadow
attend only while the sun shines.

Saying and doing have quarreled and parted.

He that's content hath enough,
He that complains has too much.

I know, young friend, Ambition fills your mind,
And in life's voyage is th'impelling wind;
But at the helm let sober reason stand,
And steer the boat with heav'n-directed hand:
So shall you safe ambition's gales receive,
and ride securely tho' the billows heave,
So shall you shun the giddy hero's fate,
and by her influence be both good and great.

When knaves betray each other
one can scarce be blamed
or the other pitied.

Silence is not always a sign of wisdom
but babbling is ever a mark of folly.

Don't overload gratitude, if you do, she'll kick.

At 20 years of age the will resigns, at 30 the wit,
at 40 the Judgement.

How few there are who have courage enough to owr
their faults, or resolution enough to mend them.

An open foe may prove a curse
but a pretended friend is worse.

When you speak to a man, look on his eyes;
when he speaks to thee, look on his mouth.

A parrot is for pratting priz'd,
But pratting women are despised;
She who attacks another's honour
Draws every living thing upon her.
Think, madam, when you stretch your lungs,
that all your neighbours too have tongues;
One slander fifty will beget;
The world with interest pays the debt.

When befriended, remember it:
When you befriend, forget it.

Strange! That a man who has wit enough
to write a satire
Should have folly enough to publish it.

1750

To the Reader,

The hope of acquireing lasting fame, is, with many authors, a most powerful motive to writing. Some, though few, have succeeded, and others, perhaps fewer, may succeed hereafter, and be as well known to posterity by their works, as the Ancients are to us. We stargazers, as ambitious to fame as any other writers whatever, after all our painful watchings and laborious calculations, have the constant mortifications to see our works thrown by at the end of the year, and treated as mere waste paper. Our only consolation is, that short-lived as they are, they outlive those of most of our contemporaries.

Yet condemned to renew the toil, we every year heave another mass up the muse's hill, which never can the summit reach, and soon comes tumbling down again.

This, kind reader, is my seventeenth labour of the kind. Through thy continued good-will, they have procured me, if no *bays,* at least *pence,* and the latter is perhaps the better of the two; since 'tis not improbable that a man may receive more solid satisfaction from pudding while he is living, than from praise after he is dead.

Thy obliged friend,

R. SAUNDERS

Father Abraham's SPEECH introduced by POOR RICHARD, *viz.*

Courteous Reader,

I have heard that nothing gives an author so great pleasure as to find his works respectfully quoted by other learned authors. This pleasure I have seldom enjoyed; for though I have been, if I may say it without vanity, an eminent author of Almanacks annually now a full quarter of a century, my brother authors in the same way, for what reason I know not, have been very sparing in their applauses; and no other author has taken the least notice of me, so that did not my writings produce me some solid *pudding,* the great deficiency of the *praise* would have quite discouraged me.

I concluded at length, that the people were the best judges of my merit; for they buy my works; and besides, in my rambles, where I am not personally known, I have frequently heard one or other of my adages repeated, with "as Poor Richard says" at the end of it. This gave me some satisfaction, as it shewed not only that my instructions were regarded, but discovered likewise some respect for my authority. And I own that, to encourage the practise of remembering and repeating those wise sentences, I have sometimes *quoted myself* with great gravity.

Judge then how much I must have been gratified by an incident I am going to relate to you. I stopped my horse lately where a great number of people were collected at a vendue of merchant goods. The hour of sale not being come, they were conversing on the badness of the time, and one of the company called to a plain clean old man, with white locks, "Pray Father Abraham, what think you of the times? Won't these heavy taxes quite ruin the country? How shall we be ever able to pay them? What would you advise us to . . . " Father Abraham stood up and replied, "If you'd have my advice, I'll give it you in short, for 'A word to the wise is enough,' and 'Many words won't fill a bushel,' as Poor Richard says." They joined in desiring him to speak his mind, and gathering around him, he proceeded as follows.

"Friends," says he, "and neighbours, the taxes are indeed very heavy, and if those laid on by the government were the only ones we had to pay, we might more easily discharge them, but we have many others, and much more grievous to some of us. We are taxed twice as much by our idleness, three times as much by our pride, and four times as much by our folly, and from these taxes the commissioners cannot ease or deliver us by allowing an abatement. However, let us harken to good advice, and something may be done for us. 'God helps them that help themselves,' as Poor Richard says in his Almanack of 1733.

"It would be thought a hard government that should tax its people one tenth of their time, to be employed in its service. But idleness taxes many of us much more, if we reckon all that is spent in absolute sloth, or doing of nothing, with that which is spent in idle employments or amusements, that amounts to nothing. Sloth, by bringing on diseases, absolutely shortens life. 'Sloth, like rust, consumes faster than labour wears, while the used key is always bright,' as Poor Richard says. How much more than is necessary do we spend in sleep! Forgetting that 'the sleeping fox catches no poultry,' and 'there will be sleeping enough in the grave,' as Poor Richard says. If time be of all things the most precious, then 'wasting time,' must be, as Poor Richard says, 'the greatest prodigality,' since, as he tells us elsewhere, 'Lost time is never found again,' and 'what we call time enough always proves little enough.' Let us then up and be doing to the purpose; so by diligence shall we do more with less perplexity. 'Sloth makes all things difficult, but industry all easy,' as Poor

Richard says; and 'He that riseth late, must trot all day, and shall scarce overtake his business at night.' While 'Laziness travels so slowly, that poverty soon overtakes him,' as we read in Poor Richard; who adds 'drive thy business; let not that drive thee'; and 'Early to bed, and early to rise, makes a man healthy, wealthy, and wise.'

"So what signifies wishing and hoping for better times. We may make these times better if we better ourselves. 'Industry need not wish,' as Poor Richard says, and 'He that lives upon hope will die fasting.' 'There are no gains without pains,' then, 'Help hands for I have no lands,' or if I have they are smartly taxed. And, as Poor Richard likewise observes, 'He that hath a trade hath an estate,' and 'He that hath a calling hath an office of profit and honour,' but then the 'trade' must be worked at, and the 'calling' well followed, or neither the 'estate' nor the 'office' will enable us to pay our taxes. If we are industrious we shall never starve; for, as Poor Richard says, 'At the working man's house hunger looks in but dares not enter.' Nor will the bailiff nor the constable enter, for 'industry pays debts, while despair increases them,' says Poor Richard. What though you have found no treasure, nor has any rich relation left you a legacy, 'Diligence is the mother of good luck,' as Poor Richard says, and 'God gives all things to industry.' Then 'plough deep, while sluggards sleep, and you shall have corn to sell and to keep,' says Poor Dick. Work while it is called today, for you know not how much you may be hindered tomorrow, which makes Poor Richard say, 'One today is worth two tomorrows,' and farther, 'Have you somewhat to do tomorrow? Do it today.' If you were a servant, would you not be ashamed that a good master should catch you idle? Are you then your own master, 'be ashamed to catch yourself idle,' as Poor Dick says. When there is so much to be done for your self, your family, your country, and your gracious King, be up by peep of day: 'Let not the sun look down and say Inglorious here he lies.' Handle your tools without mittens, remember that, 'The cat in gloves catches no mice,' as Poor Richard says. 'Tis true that there is much to be done, and perhaps you are weak handed but stick to it steadily, and you will see great effects, for 'constant dropping wears away stone,' and 'by diligence and patience the mouse ate in two the cable,' and 'little strokes fell great oaks,' as Poor Richard says in his Almanack, the Year I cannot just now remember.

"Methinks I hear some of you say, 'must a man afford himself no leisure?' I will tell thee, my friend, what Poor Richard says: 'Employ thy time well if thou meanest to gain leisure, since thou art not sure of a minute, throw not away an hour.' Leisure is time for doing something useful; this leisure the diligent man will obtain, but the lazy man never, so that, as Poor Richard says, 'a life of leisure and a life of laziness are two things.' Do you imagine that sloth will afford you more comfort than labour? No, for as Poor Richard says, 'Trouble springs from idleness, and grievous toil from needless ease. Man without labour would live by their wits only, but they break from want of stock.' Whereas industry gives comfort and plenty and respect. 'Fly from pleasures and they'll follow you. The diligent spinner has a large shift; Now I have a sheep and a cow, every body bids me good-morrow'; all which is well-said by Poor Richard.

"But with our industry we must likewise be 'steady, settled,' and 'careful,' and oversee our own affairs 'with our own eyes,' and not trust too much to others, for, as poor Richard says:

> 'I never saw an oft removed tree
> Nor yet an oft removed family,
> That throve so well as those that settled be.'

And again, 'Three removes is as bad as fire,' and again, 'Keep thy shop and thy shop will keep thee,' and again, 'If you would have your business done, go; if not, send.' And again:

> 'He that by the plough would thrive,
> Himself must either hold or drive.'

And again, 'The eye of a master will do more work than both his hands,' and again, 'Want of care does us more damage than want of knowledge,' and again, 'Not to oversee workmen is to leave them your purse open.' Trusting too much to others' care is the ruin of many, for, as the Almanack says, 'In the affairs of this world, men are saved, not by faith, but by the want of it.' but a man's own care is profitable, for, 'Learning is to the studious and riches to the careful as well as power to the bold, and heaven to the virtuous.' And farther, 'If you would have a faithful servant, and one that you like—serve yourself.' And again, he adviseth to circumspection and care, even in the smallest matters, because sometimes, 'A little neglect may breed great mischief,' adding, 'For want of a nail the shoe was lost; for want of a shoe the horse was lost; and for want of a horse the rider was lost,' being overtaken and slain by the enemy, all for want of care about a horse-shoe nail.

"So much for industry, my friends and attention to one's own business, but to these we must add frugality, if we would make our industry more certainly successful. A man may, if he knows not how to save as he gets, 'keep his nose all his life to the grindstone,' and die not worth a groat at last. 'A fat kitchen makes a lean will,' as Poor Richard says, and:

> 'Many estates are spent in the getting,
> Since women for tea forsook spinning and knitting,
> And men for punch forsook hewing and splitting.'

" 'If you would be healthy,' says he in another Almanack, 'think of saving, as well as getting: The Indies have not made Spain rich, because her outgoes are greater than her incomes.' Away then with your expensive follies, and you will not have so much cause to complain of hard times, heavy taxes, and chargeable families. For, as Poor Dick says,

> 'Women and wine, game and deceit,
> Make the wealth small, and the wants great,'

and farther, 'What maintains one vice, would bring up two children.' You may think, perhaps, that a little tea, or a little punch now and then, diet a little more costly, clothes a little finer, and a little entertainment now and then, can be no great matter, but remember what Poor Richard says, 'Many a little makes a mickle; beware of little expence, a small leak will sink a great ship: Who danties love, shall beggars prove; Fools make feasts and wise men eat them.'

"Here you are all got together at this vendue of fineries and knicknacks. You call them 'goods' but if you do not take care, they will prove 'evils' to some of you. You expect that they will be sold 'cheap,' and perhaps they may for less than they cost, but if you have no occasion for them, they must be 'dear' to you. Remember what Poor Richard says, 'Buy what thou hast no need of, and ere long thou shalt sell thy necessaries; At a great pennyworth pause a while.' He means that perhaps the cheapness is apparent only, and not real, or the bargain, by straightening thee in thy business, may do thee more harm than good. For in another place he says, 'Many have been ruined by buying good pennyworths; 'Tis foolish to lay out money in a purchase of repentence,' and yet this folly is practised every day at vendues, for want of minding the Almanack. 'Wise men learn by others harms, fools scarcely by their own.' Many a one, for the sake of finery on the back, have gone with a hungry belly, and half starved their families. 'Silks and satins, scarlet and velvets, have put out the kitchen fire.' These are not the necessaries of life, they can scarcely be called conveniences, and yet, only because they look pretty, how many want to have them. The artificial wants of mankind thus become more numerous than the natural, and, as Poor Dick says, 'For one person, there are an hundred indigent.' By these and other extravagancies the genteel are reduced to poverty, and forced to borrow of those whom they formerly despised, but who, through industry and frugality, have maintained their standing; in which case it appears plainly, that 'A ploughman on his legs is higher than a gentleman on his knees,' as Poor Richard says. Perhaps they have had a small estate left them, which they knew not the getting of; they think ' 'tis day and will never be night;' that a little to be spent out of so much, is not worth minding; 'A child and a fool,' as Poor Richard says, 'imagine twenty shillings and twenty years can never be spent; Always taking out of the meal tub and never putting in, soon comes to the bottom; When the well's dry—they know the worth of water.' But this they might have known before, if they had taken his advice. 'If you know the value of money, go and try to borrow some, for, he that goes a borrowing goes a sorrowing,' and indeed so does he that lends to such people, when he goes to get it again—Poor Dick farther advises and says,

> 'Fond pride of dress, is sure a very curse.
> E'er fancy you consult, consult your purse . . .
> Pride is as loud a beggar as want,
> and a great deal more fancy.'

When you have bought one fine thing you must buy ten more, that your appearance may be all of a piece, but Poor Dick says, ' 'Tis easier to suppress the first desire than to satisfy all that follow it.' And ' 'tis truly folly for the poor to ape the rich, as for the frog to swell in order to equal the ox.'

> 'Great estates may venture more
> But little boats should keep near shore.'

'Tis however a folly soon punished, for 'pride that dines on vanity sups on contempt,' as Poor Richard says. And, in another place, 'Pride breakfasted with plenty, dined with poverty, and supped with infamy.' And after all, of what use is this pride of appearance for which so much is risked, so much is suffered? It cannot promote health, or ease pain; it makes no increase of merit in the person, it creates envy, it hastens misfortune.

> 'What is a butterfly? At best
> He's but a caterpillar drest.
> The gaudy fop's his picture just,'

as Poor Richard says.

  "But what madness must it be to run in debt for these superfluities! We are offered by the terms of this vendue, 'six months credit,' and that perhaps has induced some of us to attend it, because we cannot spare the ready money, and hope now to be fine without it. But, ah, think what you do when you run in debt: 'You give to another power over your liberty.' If you cannot pay at the time, you will be ashamed to see your creditor; you will be in fear when you speak to him; you will make poor, pitiful, sneaking excuses, and by degrees come to loose your veracity, and sink into base downright lying; for, as Poor Richard says, 'The second vice is lying, the first is running into debt.' And again, to the same purpose, 'lying rides upon debt's back.' Whereas a freeborn Englishman ought not be ashamed or afraid to see or speak to any man living. But poverty often deprives a man of all spirit and virtue. ' 'Tis hard for an empty bag to stand upright, if it does, 'tis a stout one,' as Poor Richard truly says. What would you think of that Prince or that Government, who should issue an edict forbidding you to dress like a gentleman, or a gentlewoman, on pain of imprisonment or servitude? Would you not say that you are free, have a right to dress as you please and that such an edict would be a breach of your privileges, and such a Government tyrannical? And yet you are about 'to put yourself under that tyranny,' when you run in debt for such dress! Your creditor has authority, at his pleasure, to deprive you of your liberty, by confining you in Goal for LIFE or to SELL YOU for a servant, if you should not be able to pay him! When you have got your bargain, you may, perhaps, think little of payment, but 'creditors,' Poor Richard tells us, 'have better memories than debtors,' and in another place tells us, 'creditors are a superstitious sect—great observers of set days and times.' The Day comes round before you are aware, and the Demand is made before you are prepared to satisfy it. Or if you bear your debt in mind, the terms which at first seemed so long, will, as it lessens, appear extremely short. Time will seem to have added wings to his heels as well as shoulders. 'Those have a short Lent (saith Poor Richard) who owe money to be paid at Easter.' Then since, as he says, 'The borrower is a slave to the lender, and the debtor to the creditor,' disdain the Chain, preserve your freedom, and maintain your independency. Be industrious and free, be frugal and free. At present, perhaps, you may think yourself in

thriving circumstances, and that you can bear a little extrava-
gance without injury, but,

> 'For age and want save while you may
> No morning-sun lasts a whole day,'

as Poor Richard says. Gain may be temporary and uncertain, but
ever while you live, expence is constant and certain, and ' 'Tis
easier to build two chimnies, than to keep one in fuel,' as Poor
Richard says. So, 'Rather go to bed supperless than rise in debt.'

> 'Get what you can, and what you get hold.
> 'Tis the thing that will turn all your lead into gold,'

as Poor Richard says.

"And when you have got the Philosopher's Stone, sure you
will no longer complain of bad times, or the difficulty of paying
taxes.

"This doctrine, my friends, is reason and wisdom, but, after
all, do not depend too much upon your own industry and frugal
prudence, though excellent things, for they may all be blasted
without the blessing of heaven, and therefore ask that blessing
humbly, and be not uncharitable to those that at present seem to
want it, but comfort and help them. Remember Job suffered and
was afterwards prosperous.

"And now to conclude, 'Experience keeps a dear school, but
fools will learn in no other, and scarce in that,' for it is true, 'We
may give advice, but we cannot give conduct,' as poor Richard
says. And farther, that, 'If you will not hear and obey reason,
she'll surely rap your knuckles.' "

Thus the old gentleman ended his Harangue. The People
heard it, and approved the Doctrine and—

Immediatly practised the Contrary,

just as it had been a common Sermon, for the Vendue opened,
and they began to buy extravagantly, notwithstanding all his

cautions, and their own fear of Taxes. I found the good man had thoroughly studied my Almanacks, and digested all I had dropt on those topicks during the course of my five and twenty years. The frequent mention he made of me, must have tired any one else, but my vanity was wonderfully delighted with it, tho' I was conscious that not a tenth part of the wisdom was my own which he ascribed to me, but rather the Gleanings I had made of the sense of all Ages and Nations. However, I resolved to be the better for the Echo of it; and though I had at first determined to buy stuff for a new coat, I went away resolved to wear my old one a little longer. Reader, if thou wilt do the same, thy Profit will be as great as mine.

I am, as ever,

Thine to serve thee,

July 7, 1757.   RICHARD SAUNDERS.